# THE BATTLE OF ALCAZAR, 1594

Published @ 2017 Trieste Publishing Pty Ltd

ISBN 9780649340507

The battle of Alcazar, 1594 by George Peele



Edited by Trieste Publishing Pty Ltd.
Cover @ 2017



www.triestepublishing.com

GEORGE PEELE

# THE BATTLE OF ALCAZAR, 1594

Trieste

PRINTED FOR THE MALONE SOCIETY BY
CHARLES WHITTINGHAM & CO.
AT THE CHISWICK
PRESS

# THE BATTLE OF ALCAZAR
1594

THE MALONE SOCIETY
REPRINTS
1907

## List of Characters,

in order of entrance.

The Presenter.

Abdelmelec, uncle of the Moor.
Calsepius Bassa, Argerd Zareo, Abdil Rayes } followers of Abdelmelec.
Muly Mahamet Xeque (Seth), brother of Abdelmelec.
Rubin Arches, widow of Abdelmunen.
Muly Mahamet, the Moor.
Muly Mahamet, the younger, his son.
Pisano, his captain.
a Messenger.
a Queen.
Diego Lopis, governor of Lisbon.
an Irish Bishop.
Tom Stukley.
Jonas, Hercules } Italians in Stukley's service.
Calipolis, wife of the Moor.
Zareo, a follower of the Moor.
Sebastian, king of Portugal.
The Duke of Avero, The Duke of Barceles, Lewes de Selva, Christophero de Tavera } his followers.
Ambassadors from the Moor.
Ambassadors of Spain.
a Legate.
a Follower of Stukley (?).
Don de Menysis, governor of Tangier.
two Captains in his service.
Lord Lodowick.
Celybyn, a follower of Abdelmelec.
a Boy, serving the Moor.
a Portuguese soldier.
a Moorish soldier (?).

In the Dumb Shows.

two young Brothers of the Moor.
two Murderers.
Abdelmunen, uncle of the Moor.
three Ghosts.
Fame.

Moors, Janissaries, Ladies, Soldiers.

The names are to some extent corrupt. Muly Mahamet Xeque is called Muly Mahamet Seth in his later entrances. The two Zareos are probably due to confusion. Calipolis properly enters in I. ii, and is addressed, though she has no part in the scene (cf. l. 221, and see Plot). Lord Lodowick is addressed (l. 1052), but has no part. He is presumably the Lodevico Caesar mentioned later (l. 1114).

---

The thanks of the Society are due to Mr. A. H. Huth for information concerning his copy of the original.

# THE BATTELL OF ALCAZAR, FOVGHT

in Barbarie, betweene Sebaſtian king
of Portugall, and Abdelmelec king
of Marocco. With the
death of Captaine
*Stukeley*.

As it was ſundrie times plaid by the Lord high Admi-
rall his ſeruants.

Imprinted at London by Edward Allde for Richard
Bankworth, and are to be ſolde at his ſhoppe in
Pouls Churchyard at the ſigne of the
Sunne. 1594.

# The Tragicall battell of Alcazar in Barbarie. With the death of three Kings, and Captaine Stukley an Engliſhman.

*Enter the Preſenter.* *Act I*

HOnor the ſpurre that pricks the princely minde,
To followe rule and climbe the ſtately chaire,
With great deſire inflames the Portingall,
An honorable and couragious king,
To vndertake a dangerous dreadfull warre,
And aide with chriſtian armes the barbarous Moore,
The Negro *Muly Hames* that with-holds
The kingdome from his vnkle *Abdilmelec*,
Whom proud *Abdallas* wrongd,
And in his throne inſtals his cruell ſonne,
That now vſurps vpon this prince,
This braue Barbarian Lord *Muly Molocco*.
The paſſage to the crowne by murder made,
*Abdallas* dies, and deiſnes this tyrant king,
Of whome we treate ſprong from the Arabian moore
Blacke in his looke, and bloudie in his deeds,
And in his ſhirt ſtaind with a cloud of gore,
Preſents himſelfe with naked ſword in hand,
Accompanied as now you may behold,
With deuils coted in the ſhapes of men.

The firſt dumbe ſhew.

*Enter Muly Mahamet and his ſonne, and his two young brethren, the Moore ſheweth them the bed, and then takes his leaue of them, and they betake them to their reſt. And then the preſenter ſpeaketh.*

Like thoſe that were by kind of murther mumd,
Sit downe and ſee what hainous ſtratagems
Theſe damned wits contriue. And lo alas
How lyke poore lambes prepard for ſacrifice,
This traitor king hales to their longeſt home,
Theſe tender Lords his yonger brethren both.

The ſecond dumbe ſhew.

*Enter the Moore and two murdrers bringing in his vnkle Abdelmunen, then they draw the curtains and ſmoother the yong princes in the bed. Which done, in ſight of the vnkle they ſtrangle him in his chaire, and then goe forth. And then the Preſenter ſaith.*

His brethren thus in fatall bed behearſt,
His fathers brother of too light beleefe,
This Negro puts to death by proud command.
Saie not theſe things are faind, for true they are,
And vnderſtand how eager to inioy
His fathers crowne, this vnbeleeuing Moore
Murthering his vnkle and his brethren,
Triumphs in his ambitious tyrannie,
Till Nemiſis high miſtres of reuenge,
That with her ſcourge keepes all the world in awe,
With thundering drums awakes the God of warre,
And cals the furies from Auernus crags,
To range and rage, and vengeance to inflict
Vengeance on this accurſed Moore for ſinne,
And now behold how Abdelmelec comes,
Vnkle to this vnhappie traitor king,

Armd with great aide that *Amurath* had ſent,
Great *Amurath* Emperor of the Eaſt,
For ſeruice done to *Sultan Solimon*,
Vnder whoſe colours he had ſerud in field,
Flying the furie of this Negroes father,
That wrongd his brethren to inſtall his ſonne.
Sit you and ſee this true and tragicke warre,
A modern matter full of bloud and ruth,
Where three bolde kings confounded in their height,
Fell to the earth contending for a crowne,
And call this warre *The battell of Alcazar.* *Exit.*

*Sound Drummes and trumpets, and enter Abdilmelec* *Act I*
*with Calſepius Baſsa and his gard, and Zareo a Moore with* *sc. i*
*ſouldiers.*

*Abdel.* Alhaile Argerd Zareo and yee Moores,
Salute the frontires of your natiue home,
Ceaſe ratling drums, and Abdilmelec here
Throw vp thy trembling hands to heauens throne
Pay to thy God due thankes, and thankes to him
That ſtrengthens thee with mightie gracious armes,
Againſt the proud vſurper of thy right,
The roiall ſeate and crowne of Barbarie,
Great Amurath great Emperour of the world,
The world beare witneſſe how I do adore
The ſacred name of Amurath the great.
Calcepius Baſſa, Baſſa Calcepius
To thee and to thy truſtie band of men
That carefully attend vs in our camp,
Pickt ſouldiers comparable to the guard
Of Mermidons, that kept Achilles tent
Such thankes we giue to thee, and to them all,
As may conſerne a poore diſtreſſed king
In honour and in princely curteſie.

*Baſsa.* Curteous and honourable *Abdilmelec,*
VVe are not come at *Amuraths* command,
As merſenarie men to ſerue for pay,
But as ſure friends by our great maſter ſent
To gratifie and to remunerate,
Thy loue, thy loialtie, and forwardnes,
Thy ſeruice in his fathers dangerous warre,
And to performe in view of all the world,
The true office of right and roialtie,
To ſee thee in thy kingly chaire inthronde,
To ſettle and to ſeate thee in the ſame,
To make thee Emperor of this Barbarie,
Are come the viſeroies and ſturdie Ianiſaries
Of *Amurath,* ſonne to *Sultan Solimon.*

*Enter Muly Mahamet Xeque, Rubin Arches, Abdil Rayes, with others.*

*Abdil Rayes* Long liue my Lord the ſoueraigne of
my heart,
Lord *Abdilmelecke* whom the God of kings,
The mightie *Amurath* hath happie made,
And long liue *Amurath* for this good deed.
*Muly Mah.* Our Moores haue ſeen the ſiluer moons
to wane,
In banners brauely ſpreading ouer the plaine,
And in this ſemicircles haue deſcride
All in a golden field a ſtarre to riſe,
A glorious comet that begins to blaſe,
Promiſing happie ſorting to vs all.
*Rubyn.* Braue man at armes whom *Amurath* hath ſent
To ſow the lawfull true ſucceeding ſeed
In Barbarie, that bowes and grones withall
Vnder a proud vſurping tyrants maſe,
Right thou the wrongs this rightfull king hath borne.

*Abd.*

*Abdilm.* Diſtreſſed ladies and yee dames of Feſſe,
Sprong from the true Arabian *Muly Xarif*
The loadſtarre and the honor of our line,
Now cleere your watrie eies, wipe teares away,
And cheerfully giue welcome to theſe armes,
*Amurath* hath ſent ſcourges by his men,
To whip that tyrant traitor king from hence,
That hath vſurpt from vs, and maimd you all.
Souldiers ſith rightfull quarrels ayde
Succeſſfull are, and men that manage them
Fight not in feare as traitors and their pheres
That you may vnderſtand what armes we beare,
What lawfull armes againſt our brothers ſonne,
In fight of heauen, euen of mine honors worth,
Truly I will deliuer and diſcourſe
The ſumme of all. Deſcended from the line
Of *Mahomet*, our grandſire *Muli zaref*
With ſtore of golde and treaſure leaues Arabia,
And ſtrongly plants himſelfe in Barbary,
And of the Moores that now with vs do wend,
Our grandſire *Mulizaref* was the firſt,
From him well wot ye *Muly Mahamet Xeque*,
Who in his life time made a perfect lawe,
Confirmd with generall voice of all his peeres
That in his kingdome ſhould ſucceſsiuely
His ſonnes ſucceede. *Abdullas* was the firſt
Eldeſt of faire *Abdelmenen* the ſecond,
And we the reſt my brother and my ſelfe,
*Abdullas* raigned his time. But ſee the change,
He labours to inueſt his ſonne in all,
To diſanull the lawe our father made,
And diſ-inherite vs his brethren,
And in his life time wrongfully proclaimes,
His ſonne for king that now contends with vs,
Therefore I craue to reobtaine my right

That

That *Muly Mahamet* the traitor holdes,
Traitor and bloudie tyrant both at once,
That murthered his yonger brethren both,
But on this damned wretch, this traitor king,
The Gods ſhal poure down ſhowers of ſharp reuenge.
And thus a matter not to you vnknowen
I haue deliuered. Yet for no diſtruſt
Of loyaltie my welbeloued friend,
But that the occaſions freſh in memorie
Of theſe incumbers, ſo may moue your mindes,
As for the lawfull true ſucceeding prince,
Ye neither thinke your liues nor honors deare
Spent in a quarrell iuſt and honorable.

*Baſſa.* Such and no other we repute the cauſe,
That forwardly for thee we vndertake,
Thrice puiſant and renowmed *Abdilmelec*,
And for thine honor, ſafetie and crowne,
Our liues and honours frankly to expoſe,
To all the dangers that our warre attends,
As freely and as reſolutely all,
As anie Moore whom thou commandeſt moſt.

*Muly Xe.* And why is *Abdilmelec* then ſo ſlow
To chaſtiſe him with furie of the ſword,
Whoſe pride doth ſwell to ſway beyond his reach,
Follow this pride then with furie of reuenge.

*Rub. Ar.* Of death, of bloud, of wreake, and deepe reuenge,
Shall Rubin Archis frame her tragicke ſongs,
In bloud, in death, in murther and miſdeede,
This heauens mallice did begin and end.

*Abdilm.* Rubin theſe rights to Abdelmunens ghoſt,
Haue pearſt by this to Plutos graue below,
The bels of Pluto ring reuenge amaine,
The furies and the fiends conſpire with thee,
Warre bids me drawe my weapons for reuenge

Of

Of my deepe wrongs, and my deare brothers death.
*Muly Xe.* Sheath not your ſwords you ſoulders of Amurath,
Sheath not your ſwords you Mores of Barbary
That fight in right of your annointed king,
But follow to the gates of death and hell,
Pale death and hell to entertaine his ſoule.
Follow I ſaie to burning *Phlegiton,*
This traitor tyrant and his companies.
*Baſ.* Heaue vp your ſwords againſt theſe ſtony holds,
Wherein theſe barbarous rebels are incloſde,
Called for is Abdilmelec by the Gods,
To ſit vpon the throne of Barbarie.
*Abd. Ra.* Baſſa great thankes the honor of the Turks.
Forward braue Lords vnto this rightfull warre,
How can this battell but ſuccesfull be,
Where courage meeteth with a rightfull cauſe?
*Rub.* Go in good time my beſt beloued Lord,
Succesfull in thy worke thou vndertakes. *Exit.*

*Enter the Moore in his Chariot, attended with his ſonne.* *Act I*
*Piſano his captaine with his gard and treaſure.* *sc. ii*

*Moore. Piſano,* take a cornet of our horſe,
As many argolets and armed pikes,
And with our carriage march awaie before
By Scyras, and thoſe plots of ground
That to Moroccus leads the lower waie.
Our enemies keepe vpon the mountaine tops,
And haue incampt themſelues not farre from Feſſe,
Madame, gold is the glue, ſinewes, and ſtrength of war,
And we muſt ſee our treaſure may go ſafe,
Away.
Now boy whats the newes?
*Muly Mah.* The newes my Lord is warre, warre and

reuenge.
And if I ſhall declare the circumſtance,
Tis thus.
Rubyn our vnkles wife that wrings her hands
For Abdilmunens death, accompanied
With many dames of Feſſe in mourning weeds,
Neere to Argier encountred Abdilmelec,
That bends his force puft vp with Amuraths aide,
Againſt your holds and caſtles of defence.
The yonger brother Muly Mahamet Seth,
Greets the great Baſſa, that the king of Turkes
Sends to inuade your right and royall realme,
And baſely beg reuenge, arch-rebels all,
To be inflict vpon our progenie.
*Moore*. Why boy, is Amuraths Baſsa ſuch a bug,
That he is markt to do this doubtie deed?
Then Baſſa locke the winds in wards of braſſe,
Thunder from heauen damne wretched men to death
Barre all the offices of Saturnes ſonnes,
Be Pluto then in hell and barre the fiends,
Take Neptunes force to thee and calme the ſeas,
And execute Ioues iuſtice on the world,
Conuey Tamberlaine into our Affrike here,
To chaſtice and to menace lawfull kings,
Tamberlaine triumph not, for thou muſt die
As Philip did, Cæſar, and Cæſars peeres.
*Muly Mah*. The Baſſa groſly flattered to his face,
And Amuraths praiſe aduancde aboue the ſound
Vpon the plaines, the ſouldiers being ſpread,
And that braue gard of ſturdie Ianizaries,
That Amurath to Abdilmelec gaue,
And bad him boldly be to them as ſafe,
As if he ſlept within a walled towne,
Who take them to their weapons threatning reuenge.
Bloudie reuenge, bloudie reuengefull warre.

*Moore*.

*Moore.* Awaie, and let me heare no more of this,
Why boy, are we ſucceſſours to the great Abdilmelec,
Deſcended from the Arabian Muly Zarif,
And ſhall we be afraide of Baſſas and of bugs,
Rawe head and bloudie bone?
Boy, ſeeſt here this ſemitarie by my ſide,
Sith they begin to bath in blond,
Bloud be the theame whereon our time ſhall tread,
Such ſlaughter with my weapon ſhall I make,
As through the ſtreame and bloudie chanels deepe,
Our Moores ſhall ſaile in ſhips and pinnaces,
From Tanger ſhore vnto the gates of Feſſe.
*Muly Mah.* And of thoſe ſlaughtered bodies ſhall thy ſonne,
A huge towre erect like Nemrods frame,
To threaten thoſe vniuſt and parciall Gods,
That to Abdallas lawfull ſeed denie,
A long, a happie, and triumphant raigne.

Sound an alarum within, and enter a meſſenger.

*Meſ.* Flie king of Feſſe, king of Moroccus flie,
Flie with thy friends Emperour of Barbary,
O flie the ſword and furie of the foe,
That rageth as the ramping lyoneſſe,
In reſcue of her yonglings from the beare,
Thy townes and holds by numbers baſely yeeld,
Thy land to Abdilmelecs rule reſignes,
Thy carriage and thy treaſure taken is
By Amuraths ſouldiers, that haue ſworne thy death,
Flie Amuraths power, and Abdilmelecs threats,
Or thou and thine looke heere to breath your laſt.
*More.* Villain, what dreadfull ſound of death & flight
Is this, wherewith thou doeſt afflict our eares?
But if there be no ſafetie to abide

The fauor, fortune, and ſucceſſe of warre.
Away in haſt, roule on my chariot wheeles
Reſtleſſe, till I be ſafely ſet in ſhade
Of ſome vnhanted place, ſome blaſted groue
Of deadly hue, or diſmall cypres tree,
Farre from the light or comfort of the Sunne,
There to curſe heauen, and he that heaues me hence,
To ſeeke as Enuie at Cecropes gate,
And pine the thought and terrour of miſhaps,
Awaie. *Exit.*

## *Act II* *Actus ſecunda. Scæna prima.*

Alarum.
And then the preſenter ſpeaketh.

Now warre begins his rage and ruthleſſe raine,
And Nemiſis with bloudie whip in hand,
Thunders for vengeance on this Negro moore.
Nor may the ſilence of the ſpeechleſſe night,
Diuine Architects of murthers and miſdeeds,
Of tragedies, and tragicke tyrannies,
Hide or containe this barbarous crueltie
Of this vſurper to his progenie.

*Three ghoſts crying* Vindicta.

Hearke Lords, as in a hollow place a farre,
The dreadfull ſhrikes and clamors that reſound,
And ſound reuenge vpon this traitors ſoule,
Traitor to kinne and kinde, to Gods and men.
Now Nemiſis vpon her doubling drum,
Moude with this gaſtly mone, this ſad complaint,
Larumes aloud into Alectos eares,
And with her thundering wakes whereas they lie,
In caue as darke as hell, and beds of ſteele,
The furies iuſt impes of dire reuenge,

Reuenge cries Abdilmelecs grieued ghoſt,
And rouſeth with the terror of this noiſe
Theſe nymphs of Erybus. Wreake and reuenge
Ring out the ſoules of his vnhappie brethren,
And now ſtart vp theſe torments of the world,
Wakt with the thunder of Ramuſians drum,
And feareful ecchos of theſe grieued ghoſts,
Alecto with her brand and bloudie torch,
Megæra with her whip and ſnakie haire,
Tyſiphone with her fatall murthering yron,
Theſe three conſpire, theſe three complaine & mone,
Thus Muly Mahamet is a counſell held,
To wreake the wrongs and murthers thou haſt done.
By this imagine was this barbarous Moore
Chaſed from his dignitie and his diademe,
And liues forlorne among the mountaine ſhrubs,
And makes his food the fleſh of ſauage beaſts.
Amureths ſouldiers haue by this inſtald
Good Abdelmelec in his roiall ſeate,
The dames of Feſſe and ladies of the land,
In honor of the ſonne of Soliman,
Erect a ſtatue made of beaten gold,
And ſing to Amurath ſongs of laſting praiſe.
Muly Mahamets furie ouer-rulde,
His crueltie controld, and pride rebukt,
Now at laſt when ſober thoughts renude,
Care of his kingdome and deſired crowne,
The aide that once was offered and refusde
By meſſengers, he furiouſly imployes,
Sebaſtians aide braue king of Portugall,
He forward in all armes and chiualrie
Hearkens to his Embaſſadors, and grants
What they in letters and by words intreate.
Now liſten lordings now begins the game,

Sebaſtians tragedie in this tragicke warre.

*Act II sc. i* Alarum within, and then enter Abdilmelec, Muly Mahamet Seth, Calſepius Baſſa, with Moores and Ianizaries, and the Ladies.

*Abdil.* Now hath the Sun diſplaid his golden beams,
And duskie clouds diſpearſt, the welkin cleeres,
Wherein the twentie coloured rainbow ſhewes,
After this fight happie and fortunate,
Wherein our Moores haue loſt the day,
And victorie adornd with fortunes plumes,
Alights on Abdelmelecs glorious creaſt,
Here finde we time to breath, and now begin
To paie thy due and duties thou doeſt owe,
To heauen and earth, to Gods and Amurath.
Sound Trumpets.
And now drawe neere, and heauen and earth giue eare
Giue eare and record heauen and earth with me,
Ye Lords of Barbarie hearken and attend,
Hearke to the wordes I ſpeake, and vowe I make,
To plant the true ſuccesſion of the crowne,
Loe Lords, in our ſeate roiall to ſucceede,
Our onely brother here we doo inſtall,
And by the name of Muly Mahamet Seth,
Intitle him true heire vnto the crowne,
Ye Gods of heauen gratulate this deed,
That men on earth may therwith ſtand content.
Lo thus my due and duetie is done, I paie
To heauen and earth, to Gods and Amurath.
Sound Trumpets.
*Muly Mah.* Renowmed Baſſa, to remunerate
Thy worthines and magnanimitie,
Behold the nobleſt ladies of the land,
Bring preſent tokens of their gratitude.

*Rub. Ar.* Rubin that breaths but for reuenge,
Baſſa by this commends her ſelfe to thee
Reſigne the token of her thankfulnes
To Amurath the God of earthly kings,
Doth Rubin giue and ſacrifice her ſonne,
Not with ſweet ſmoake of fire, or ſweet perfume,
But with his fathers ſword, his mothers thankes
Doth Rubin giue her ſonne to Amurath.

*Queene.* As Rubin giues her ſonne, ſo we our ſelues
To Amurath giue, and fall before his face.
Baſſa, weare thou the golde of Barbarie,
And gliſter like the pallace of the Sunne,
In honour of the deed that thou haſt dun.

*Baſ.* Well worthie of the aide of Amurath,
Is Abdilmelec and theſe noble dames,
Rubin thy ſonne I ſhall ere long beſtow,
Where thou doeſt him bequeath in honours fee,
On Amurath, mightie Emperor of the Eaſt,
That ſhall receiue the impe of roiall race,
With cheerefull lookes and gleames of princely grace,
This choſen gard of Amuraths Ienizaries,
I leaue to honor and attend on thee,
King of Marocco conqueror of thy foes,
True king of Feſſe, Emperor of Barbarie,
Muly Molocco liue and keepe thy ſeate,
In ſpite of fortunes ſpite or enemies threats,
Ride Baſſa now, bold Baſsa homeward ride,
As glorious as great Pompey in his pride.

*Exit omnes.*

*Enter Diego Lopis gouernor of Lisborne, the Iriſh Biſhop, Stukley, Ionas, and Hercules.* *Act II sc. ii.*

*Dieg.* Welcome to Lisborne valiant Catholikes,
Welcome braue Engliſh-men to Portugall,
Moſt reuerent primate of the Iriſh Church.

And

And noble *Stukeley* famous by thy name,
Welcome, thrice welcome to Sebaſtians towne,
And welcome Engliſh captaines to you all,
It ioyeth vs to ſee his holynes fleet,
Caſt ancor happily vpon our coaſt.
*Biſhop*. Theſe welcomes worthie gouernor of Liſborne,
Argue an honorable minde in thee,
But treate of our misfortune therewithall,
To Ireland by pope Gregories command,
Were we all bound, and therefore thus imbarkt,
To land our forces there at vnawares,
Conquering the land for his holyneſſe,
And ſo reſtore it to the Romane faith,
This was the cauſe of our expedition,
And Ireland long ere this had bin ſubdude,
Had not foule weather brought vs to this bay.
*Diego*. Vnder correction, are ye not all Engliſhmen,
And longs not Ireland to that kingdome Lords?
Then may I ſpeake my conſcience in the cauſe,
Sance ſcandall to the holy ſea of Rome,
Vnhonorable is this expedition,
And misbeſeeming yoo to meddle in.
*Stuk*. Lord gouernour of Lisborne vnderſtand,
As we are Engliſhmen, ſo are we men,
And I am Stukley ſo reſolude in all,
To follow rule, honor and Emperie,
Not to be bent ſo ſtrictly to the place,
Wherein at firſt I blew the fire of life,
But that I may at libertie make choiſe,
Of all the continents that bounds the world,
For why? I make it not ſo great deſert
To be begot or borne in anie place,
Sith thats a thing of pleaſure and of eaſe,
That might haue bin performd elſe-where as well.

*Die.* Follow what your good pleaſure will,
Good Captaine Stukley be it farre from me
To take exceptions beyond my priuiledge.
*Biſh.* Yet captaine giue me leaue to ſpeake,
We muſt affect our countrie as our parents,
And if at anie time we alianate
Our loue or induſtrie from doing it honor,
It muſt reſpect effects and touch the ſoule,
Matter of conſcience and religion,
And not deſire of rule or benefite.
*Stuk.* Well ſaid Biſhop, ſpoken like your ſelfe,
The reuerent lordly biſhop of ſaint Aſſes.
*Herc.* The biſhop talkes according to his coate,
And takes not meaſure of it by his minde,
You ſee he hath it made thus large and wide,
Becauſe he may conuert it as he liſt,
To anie forme may fit the faſhion beſt,
*Biſh.* Captaine you do me wrong to deſcant thus,
Vpon my coate or double conſcience,
And cannot anſwere it in another place.
*Die.* Tis but in ieſt, Lord biſhop put it vp,
And all as friends daine to be entertaind,
As my abilitie here can make prouiſion,
Shortly ſhall I conduct you to the king,
Whoſe welcomes euermore to ſtrangers are,
Princely and honorable as his ſtate becomes.
*Stuk.* Thankes worthie gouernor, come biſhop come
Will you ſhew fruits of quarrell and of wrath,
Come let vs in with my Lord of Lisborne here.
And put all conſcience into one carouſe,
Letting it out againe, as we may liue.
There ſhall no action paſse my hand or ſword,
That cannot make a ſtep to gaine a crowne,
No word ſhall paſſe the office of my tong,
That ſounds not of affection to a crowne,

No thought haue being in my lordly breſt,
That workes not euerie waie to win a crowne,
Deeds, wordes and thoughts ſhall all be as a kings,
My chiefeſt companie ſhall be with kings,
And my deſerts ſhall counterpoiſe a kings,
Why ſhould not I then looke to be a king?
I am the marques now of Ireland made,
And will be ſhortly king of Ireland,
King of a mole-hill had I rather be,
Than the richeſt ſubiect of a monarchie,
Huffe it braue minde, and neuer ceaſe t'aſpire,
Before thou raigne ſole king of thy deſire. *Exeunt.*

*Act II sc. iii* *Enter the Moore, with Calipolis his wife, Muly Mahamet his ſonne, and two others.*

*Moore.* Where art thou boy, where is Calypolis?
O deadly wonnd that paſſeth by mine eie,
The fatall priſon of my ſwelling heart!
O fortune conſtant in vnconſtancie!
Fight earth-quakes in the intrailes of the earth,
And Eaſterne whirl-windes in the helliſh ſhades,
Some foule contagion of the infected heauen,
Blaſt all the trees, and in their curſed tops,
The diſmall night rauen and tragike owle
Breed, and become fore-tellers of my fall,
The fatall ruine of my name and me,
Adders and ſerpents hiſſe at my diſgrace,
And wound the earth with anguiſh of their ſtings,
Now Abdelmelec, now triumph in Feſſe,
Fortune hath made thee king of Barbary.

*Caly.* Alas my Lord, what boots theſe huge exclaims
To aduantage vs in this diſtreſt eſtate,
O pittie our perplext eſtate my Lord,
And turne all curſes to ſubmiſſe complaints,
And thoſe complaints to actions of reliefe,
I faint my Lord, and naught may curſing plaintes

Refreſh

Refresh the fading substance of my life.
*Moore.* Faint all the world, consume and be accurst,
Since my state faints and is accurst.
*Calyp.* Yet patience Lord to conquere sorrowes so.
*More.* What patience is for him that lacks his crown?
There is no patience where the losse is such,
The shame of my disgrace hath put on wings,
And swiftly flies about this earthly ball,
Car'st thou to liue then fond Calypolis,
When he that should giue essence to thy soule,
He on whose glorie all thy ioy should stay,
Is soulelesse, glorylesse, and desperate,
Crying for battell, famine, sword and fire,
Rather then calling for reliefe or life.
But be content, thy hunger shall haue end,
Famine shall pine to death and thou shalt liue,
I will go hunt these cursed solitaries,
And make the sword and target here my hound,
To pull downe lyons and vntamed beasts. *Exit.*
*Mab.* Tush mother, cherish your vnheartie soule,
And feede with hope of happines and ease,
For if by valor or by policie,
My kingly father can be fortunate,
We shall be Ioues commanders once againe,
And flourish in a three-fold happines.
*Zareo* His maiestie hath sent Sebastian
The good and harmelesse king of Portugall,
A promise to resigne the roialtie
And kingdome of Marocco to his hands,
But when this haughtie offer takes effect,
And workes affiance in Sebastian,
My gracious Lord warnd wisely to aduise,
I doubt not but will watch occasion,
And take her fore-top by the slenderest haire,
To rid vs of this miserable life.

*Mab.* Good madame cheere your ſelfe, my Fathers wife,
He can ſubmit himſelfe and liue below,
Make ſhew of friendſhip, promiſe, vow and ſweare,
Till by the vertue of his faire pretence,
Sebaſtian truſting his integritie,
He makes himſelfe poſſeſsor of ſuch fruits,
As grow vpon ſuch great aduantages.
*Calip.* But more diſhonor hangs on ſuch miſdeeds,
Than all the profit their returne can beare,
Such ſecret iudgements hath the heauens impoſde
Vpon the drouping ſtate of Barbarie,
As publike merites in ſuch lewd attempts,
Hath drawne with violence vpon our heads.

*Enter Muly Mahamet with lyons fleſh vpon his ſworde.*

*Mu. Ma.* Hold thee Calypolis feed and faint no more,
This fleſh I forced from a lyoneſſe,
Meate of a princeſſe, for a princeſſe meate,
Learne by her noble ſtomacke to eſteeme
Penurie plentie, in extreameſt dearth,
Who when ſhe ſawe her foragement bereft,
Pinde not in melancholy or childliſh feare,
But as braue mindes are ſtrongeſt in extreames,
So ſhe redoubling her former force
Rangde thorough the woodes, and rent the breeding vaultes
Of proudeſt ſauages to ſaue her ſelfe,
Feede then and faint not faire Calypolis,
For rather than fierce famine ſhall preuaile,
To gnaw thy intrailes with her thornie teeth,
The conquering lyoneſſe ſhall attend on thee,
And laie huge heapes of ſlaughtered carcaſes

As

As bulwarkes in her waie to keepe her backe.
I will prouide thee of a princely oſpraie,
That as ſhe flyeth ouer fiſh in pooles,
The fiſh ſhall turne their gliſtering bellies vp,
And thou ſhalt take thy liberall choice of all,
Ioues ſtately bird with wide commanding wings
Shall houer ſtill about thy princely head,
And beate downe fowle by ſholes into thy lap,
Feede then and faint not faire Calypolis.

*Calyp.* Thankes good my Lord, and though my ſto-
macke be
Too queaſie to diſgeſt ſuch bloudie meate,
Yet ſtrength I it with vertue of my minde,
I doubt no whit but I ſhall liue my Lord.

*Moore.* Into the ſhades then faire Calypolis,
And make thy ſonne and Negros here good cheere,
Feede and be fat that we may meete the foe
With ſtrength and terror to reuenge our wrong.

*Enter Sebaſtian king of Portugall, the Duke of Auero, the duke of Barceles, Leues de Silua, Chriſtophero de Tauera* Act II sc. iv

*Sebaſt.* Call forth thoſe Moores, thoſe men of Bar-
barie,
That came with letters from the king of Feſſe.
*Exit one.*
Ye warlike lords and men of chiualrie,
Honorable Embaſſadors of this high regent,
Harke to Sebaſtian king of Portugall:
Theſe letters ſent from your diſtreſſed Lord,
Torne from his throne by Abdilmelecs hand,
Strengthned and raiſde by furious Amurath,
Imports a kingly fauor at our hands,
For aide to reobtaine his roiall ſeate,
And place his fortunes in their former height.

For quitall of which honorable armes,
By theſe his letters he doth firmely vow,
Wholy to yeeld and to ſurrender vp
The kingdome of Maroccus to our hands,
And to become to vs contributarie,
And to content himſelfe with the realme of Feſſe,
Theſe lines my Lords writ in extremitie,
Containe therefore but during fortunes date,
How ſhall Sebaſtian then beleeue the ſame?
*Embaſ.* Viceroies, and moſt chriſtian king of Portugall,
To ſatisfie thy doubtfull minde heerein,
Command forthwith a blaſing brand of fire
Be brought in preſence of thy maieſtie,
Then ſhalt thou ſee by our religious vowes
And ceremonies moſt inuiolate
How firme our ſoueraignes proteſtations are,
Beholde my Lord, this bindes our faith to thee,
In token that great Muly Mahamets hand
Hath writ no more than his ſtout heart allowes,
And will performe to thee and to thine heires,
We offer heere our hands into this flame,
And as this flame doth faſten on this fleſh,
So from our ſoules we wiſh it may conſume
The heart of our great Lord and ſoueraigne
Muly Mahamet king of Barbarie,
If his intent agree not with his wordes.
*Sebaſt.* Theſe ceremonies and proteſtations
Sufficeth vs ye Lordes of Barbarie,
Therefore returne this anſwere to your king,
Aſſure him by the honour of my crowne,
And by Sebaſtians true vnfained faith
He ſhall haue aide and ſuccour to recouer,
And ſeate him in his former emperie,
Let him relie vpon our princely word,

Tell him by Auguſt we will come to him,
With ſuch a power of braue impatient mindes,
As Abdelmelec and great Amurath
Shall tremble at the ſtrength of Portugall.
*Emb.* Thanks to the renowmed king of Portugal
On whoſe ſtout promiſes our ſtate depend.
*Sebaſt.* Barbarians go glad your diſtreſſed king,
And ſaie Sebaſtian liues to right his wrong, *Exit.*
Duke of Auero call in thoſe Engliſh-men,
Don Stukley, and thoſe Captaines of the fleet
That lately landed in our bay of Lisborne.
Now breath Sebaſtian, and in breathing blow
Some gentle gale of thy new formed ioyes,
Duke of Auero, it ſhall be your charge,
To take the muſter of the Portugals,
And braueſt blouds of all our countrie,
Lewes de Sylua you ſhall be diſpatcht
With letters vnto Philip king of Spaine,
Tell him we craue his aide in this behalfe,
I know our brother Philip nill denie
His furtherance in this holy chriſtian warre,
Duke of Barceles as thy anceſtors
Haue alwaies loiall bin to Portugall,
So now in honor of thy toward youth,
Thy charge ſhall be to Anwerpe ſpeedily,
To hire vs mercenarie men at armes,
Promiſe them princely paie, and be thou ſure
Thy word is ours, Sebaſtian ſpeakes the word.
*Chri.* I beſeech your maieſtie imploy me in this war.
*Seb.* Chriſtopher de Tauera, next vnto my ſelfe
My good Efeſtian, and my bedfellow,
Thy cares and mine ſhall be alike in this,
Enter Stukley and the reſt.
And thou and I will liue and die together.
And now braue Engliſh-men to you,

Whom angrie ſtormes haue put into our bay,
Hold not your fortune ere the worſe in this,
We holde our ſtrangers honors in our hand,
And for diſtreſſed franke and free reliefe,
Tell me then Stukley, for thats thy name I trow,
Wilt thou in honor of thy countries fame,
Hazard thy perſon in this braue exploit,
And follow vs to fruitfull Barbarie,
With theſe ſixe thouſand ſouldiers thou haſt brought
And choicely pickt through wanton Italy,
Thou art a man of gallant perſonage,
Proud in thy lookes, and famous euerie waie,
Frankly tell me, wilt thou go with me?
*Stuk.* Couragious king, the wonder of my thoughts
And yet my Lord, with pardon vnderſtand,
My ſelfe and theſe, whom weather hath inforſt,
To lie at roade vpon thy gracious coaſt,
Did bend our courſe and made amaine for Ireland.
*Sebaſt.* For Ireland Stukley, thou miſtakſt me wonderous much,
With ſeuen ſhippes, two pinnaces, and ſixe thouſand men,
I tell thee Stukley, they are farre too weake,
To violate the Queene of Irelands right,
For Irelands Queene commandeth Englands force,
Were euerie ſhip ten thouſand on the ſeas,
Mand with the ſtrength of all the Eaſterne kings,
Conuaying all the monarchs of the world,
To inuade the Iland where her highnes raignes,
Twere all in vaine, for heauens and deſtinies
Attend and wait vpon her Maieſtie,
Sacred, imperiall, and holy is her ſeate,
Shining with wiſedome, loue and mightines.
Nature that euerie thing imperfect made,
Fortune that neuer yet was conſtant found,

Time

Time that defaceth euerie golden ſhew,
Dare not decay, remoue, or be impure,
Both nature, time and fortune, all agree,
To bleſſe and ſerue her roiall maieſtie,
The wallowing Ocean hems her round about,
Whoſe raging flouds do ſwallow vp her foes,
And on the rockes their ſhips in peeces ſplit,
And euen in Spaine where all the traitors dance,
And plaie themſelues vpon a ſunny daie,
Securely gard the weſt part of her Iſle,
The South the narow Britaine ſea begirts,
Where Veptune ſits in triumph, to direct
Their courſe to hell that aime at her diſgrace,
The Germaine ſeas alongſt the Eaſt do run,
Where Nenus banquets all her water Nymphs,
That with her beautie glanſing on the waues,
Diſdaines the checke of faire Proſerpina,
Aduiſe thee then proud Stukley ere thou paſſe,
To wrong the wonder of the higheſt God,
Sith danger, death and hell doth follow thee,
Thee and them all that ſeeke to danger her.
If honor be the marke wherat thou aimſt,
Then followe me in holy chriſtian warres,
And leaue to ſeeke thy Countries ouerthrow.
*Stuk*. Rather my Lord, let me admire theſe wordes,
Than anſwere to your firme obiections,
His holynes Pope Gregorie the ſeuenth,
Hath made vs foure the leaders of the reſt,
Amongſt the reſt my Lord, I am but one,
If they agree, Stukley will be the firſt
To die with honor for Sebaſtian.
*Sebaſt*. Tell me Lord Biſhop, Captaines tell me all,
Are you content to leaue this enterpriſe,
Againſt your countrie and your countrie men,
To aide Mahamet king of Barbarie?

*Bish.* To aide Mahamet king of Barbarie,
Tis gainst our vowes great king of Portugall.
*Sebast.* Then Captaines what saie you?
*Jonas* I saie my Lord as the Bishop said,
We may not turne from conquering Ireland.
*Herc.* Our countrie and our country-men will condemne
Vs worthie of death, if we neglect our vowes.
*Sebast.* Consider Lords you are now in Portugall,
And I may now dispose of you and yours.
Hath not the winde and weather giuen you vp,
And made you captiues to our roiall will?
*Ionas.* It hath my Lord, and willingly wee yeeld
To be commanded by your maiestie,
But if you make vs voluntarie men,
Our course is then direct for Ireland.
*Sebast.* That course will we direct for Barbary,
Follow me Lords, Sebastian leades the way,
To plant the christian fath in Affrica.
*Stuk.* Saint George for England, and Irelande nowe adue,
For here Tom Stukley shapes his course anue.
*Exit.*

*Act III* *Enter the presenter and speakes.*

Lo thus into a lake of bloud and gore,
The braue couragious king of Portugall
Hath drencht himselfe, and now prepares amaine
With sailes and oares to crosse the swelling seas,
With men and ships, courage and canon shot,
To plant this cursed Moore in fatall houre,
And in this Catholike case the king of Spaine
Is cald vpon by sweet Sebastian.
Who surfetting in prime time of his youth,

Vpon

Vpon ambitious poiſon dies thereon.
By this time is the Moore to Tangar come,
A citie longing to the Portugall,
And now doth Spaine promiſe with holy face,
As fauouring the honor of the cauſe,
His aide of armes, and leuies men apace,
But nothing leſſe than king Sebaſtians good
He meanes, yet at Sucor de Tupea,
He met ſome ſaie in perſon with the Portugall,
And treateth of a marriage with the king,
But ware ambitious wiles and poiſned eies,
There was nor aide of armes nor marriage,
For on his waie without thoſe Spaniardes king Seba-
ſtian went.

*Enter the king of Portugall and his Lordes, Lewes de Syl-ua, and the Embaſsadors of Spaine.* *Act III sc. i*

*Seb.* Honorable Lords, Embaſſadors of Spaine,
The many fauors by our meetings done
From our beloued and renowmed brother,
Philip the Catholike king of Spaine
Say therefore good my Lord Embaſſador,
Saie how your mightie maſter minded is,
To propagate the fame of Portugall.
*Embaſ.* To propagate the fame of Portugall,
And plant religious truth in Affrica,
Philip the great and puiſant king of Spaine,
For loue and honor of Sebaſtians name,
Promiſeth aide of armes, and ſweares by vs
To doe your maieſtie all the good he can,
With men, munition, and ſupply of warre,
Of Spaniards proud in king Sebaſtians aide,

To ſpend their blouds in honor of their Chriſt.
*Legate.* And farther to manifeſt vnto your maieſty
How much the Catholike king of Spaine affects
This warre with Moores and men of little faith,
The honour of your euerlaſting praiſe,
Behold to honor and inlarge thy name,
He maketh offer of his daughter Iſabel,
To linke in marriage with the braue Sebaſtian,
And to inrich Sebaſtians noble wife,
His maieſtie with promiſe to reſigne
The titles of the Iſlands of Moloccus,
That by his roialtie in Iudah he commands
Theſe fauors with vnfained loue and zeale,
Voweth king Philip to king Sebaſtian.
*Sebaſt.* And God ſo deale with king Sebaſtians ſoul
As iuſtly he intends to fight for Chriſt,
Nobles of Spaine, ſith our renowmed brother,
Philip the king of honor and of zeale,
By you the choſen Orators of Spaine,
The offer of the holdes he makes
Are not ſo precious in our account,
As is the peerleſſe dame whom we adore,
His daughter, in whoſe loyaltie conſiſts
The life and honor of Sebaſtian.
As for the aide of armes he promiſeth,
We will expect, and thankfully receiue
At Cardis, as we ſaile alongſt the coaſt.
Sebaſtian clap thy hands for ioy,
Honourd by this meeting and this match,
Go Lords and follow to the famous warre
Your king, and be his fortune ſuch in all,
As he intends to manage armes in right.
*Exeunt.*
*Manet Stukley and another.*
*Stuk.* Sit faſt Sebaſtian, and in this worke

God

God and good men labor for Portugall,
For Spaine diſguiſing with a double face,
Flatters thy youth and forwardnes good king,
Philip whome ſome call the catholike king,
I feare me much thy faith will not be firme,
But diſagree with thy profeſsion.
*The other.* What then ſhall of theſe men of warre become,
Thoſe numbers that do multiply in Spaine?
*Stuk.* Spaine hath a vent for them and their ſupplies,
The Spaniard readie to imbarke himſelfe,
Heere gathers to a head, but all to ſure,
Flanders I feare ſhall feele the force of Spaine,
Let Portugall fare as he may or can,
Spaine meanes to ſpend no pouder on the moores.
*The other.* If kings doo dally ſo with holy oaths,
The heauens will right the wrongs that they ſuſtaine,
Philip if theſe forgeries be in thee,
Aſſure thee king, twill light on thee at laſt,
And when proud Spaine hopes ſoundly to preuaile,
The time may come that thou and thine ſhall faile.
*Exit.*

*Enter Abdelmelec, Muly Mahamet Seth, Zareo and their Traine.* *Act III sc. ii*

*Abdelm.* The Portugall lead with deceiuing hope,
Hath raiſde his power, and receiu'd our foe
With honorable welcomes and regard,
And left his countrie bounds, and hether bends,
In hope to helpe Mahamet to a crowne,
And chaſe vs hence, and plant this Negro moore
That clads himſelfe in coat of hammerd ſteele,
To heaue vs from the honor we poſſeſſe,
But for I haue my ſelfe a ſouldier bin,

I haue in pittie to the *Portugall*
Sent ſecret meſſengers to counſell him.
As for the aide of Spaine whereof they hop'd,
We haue diſpatcht our letters to their prince,
To craue that in a quarrell ſo vniuſt,
He that intituled is the Catholike king,
Would not aſsiſt a careleſſe chriſtian prince,
And as by letters we are let to know,
Our offer of the ſeuen holdes we made,
He thankfully receines, with all conditions,
Differing in minde farre from all his wordes
And promiſes to king Sebaſtian,
As we would wiſh, or you my Lords deſire.
*Zareo.* What reſteth then but Abdelmelec may
Beate backe this proud inuading *Portugall,*
And chaſtice this ambitious Negro moore
With thouſand deaths for thouſand damned deeds.
*Abdilm.* Forward Zareo and ye manly moores,
Sebaſtian ſee in time vnto thy ſelfe,
If thou and thine miſled doe thriue amiſſe,
Guiltleſſe is Abdilmelec of thy bloud.
*Exeunt.*

*Act III sc. iii*

*Enter Don de Menyſis gouernor of Tangar, with his companie ſpeaking to the Captaine.*

*Gouer.* Captaine, we haue receiued Letters from the king,
That with ſuch ſignes and arguments of loue,
We entertaine the king of Barbarie,
That marcheth toward Tangar with his men,
The poore remainders of thoſe that fled from Feſſe,
When Abdilmelec got the glorious day,
And ſtald himſelfe in his emperiall throne.
*Cap.* Lord gouernor, we are in readines
To welcome and receiue this hapleſſe king,

Chaſed

Chaſed from his land by angrie Amurath,
And if the right reſt in this luſtie Moore,
Bearing a princely heart vnvanquiſhable,
A noble reſolution than it is,
In braue Sebaſtian our chriſtian king,
To aide this Moore with his victorious armes,
Thereby to propagate religious truth,
And plant his ſpringing praiſe in Affrica.

*Ano. Capt.* But when ariues this braue Sebaſtian,
To knit his forces with this manly Moore,
That both in one, and one in both may ioyne
In this attempt of noble conſequence?
Our men of Tangar long to ſee their king,
Whoſe princely face that lyke the ſummers ſonne,
Glads all theſe hether parts of Barbarie.

*Gouern.* Captaines, he commeth hetherward amaine,
Top and top gallant, all in braue araie
The 26. daie of Iune he lefte the bay of Lisborne,
And with all his fleete at Cardis happily he
Ariu'de in Spain the eight of Iuly, tarrying for the aide
That *Philip* king of Spaine had promiſed,
And fifteene daies he there remaind aboord,
Expecting when this Spaniſh force would come,
Nor ſtept a ſhore as he were going ſtill:
But Spaine that meant and minded nothing leſſe,
pretends a ſodaine feare and care to keepe
His owne from Amuraths fierce inuaſion,
And to excuſe his promiſe to our king,
For which he ſtormes as great Achilles earſt.
Lying for want of winde in Aldeſt gulfe,
And hoiſeth vp his ſailes, and anchors waighs,
And hetherward he comes, and lookes to meete
This manly Moore, whoſe caſe he vndertakes,
Therefore go we to welcome and reſcue,
With canon ſhot, and ſhouts of yong and olde,

This fleet of Portugals and troupe of Moores.
*Exit.*

*Act III sc. iv*

*The Trumpets sound, the chambers are dischargde. Then enter the king of Portugall and the Moore, with all theyr traine.*

*Sebast.* Muly Mahamet king of Barbarie
Well met, and welcome to our towne of Tanger,
After this sodaine shocke and haplesse warre,
Welcome braue Queene of Moores, repose thee here,
Thou and thy noble sonne, and souldiers all,
Ropose you here in king Sebastians towne.
Thus farre in honor of thy name and aide
Lord Mahamet, we haue aduentured
To winne for thee a kingdome, for our selues
Fame, and performance of those promises,
That in thy faith and roialtie thou hast
Sworne to Sebastian king of *Portugall*,
And thriue it so with thee as thou doest meane,
And meane thou so as thou doest wish to thriue,
And if our Christ for whom in chiefe we fight,
Heereby to inlarge the bounds of christendome,
Fauor this warre, and as I do not doubt,
Send victorie to light vpon my crest.
Braue Moore I will aduance thy kingly sonne,
And with a diademe of pearle and golde,
Adorne thy temples and inrich thy head,
*Moore* O braue Sebastian noble *Portugall*,
Renowmd and honourd euer maist thou bee,
Triumpher ouer those that menace thee.
The hellish prince grim *Pluto* with his mace
Ding downe my soule to hel, and with this soule
This sonne of mine, the honor of my house,
But I performe religiously to thee,

That

That I haue holyly earſt vndertane,
And that thy Lords and Captaines may perceiue
My minde in this ſingle and pure to be,
As pure as is the water of the brooke,
My deareſt ſonne to thee I doo ingage,
Receiue him Lord in hoſtage of my vow,
For euen my minde preſageth to my ſelfe,
That in ſome ſlauiſh ſort I ſhall beholde
Him dragde along this running riuer ſhore,
A ſpectacle to dant the pride of thoſe
That climbe aloft by force, and not by right.

*The Moores ſonne.* Nor can it otherwiſe befall the man
That keeps his ſeate and ſcepter all in feare,
That weares his crowne in eie of all the world,
Reputed theft and not inheritance.
What title then hath Abdilmelec here,
To barre our father or his progenie,
Right roiall prince, hereof you make no doubt,
Agreeing with your wholſome chriſtian lawes,
Helpe then couragious Lord with hand and ſword,
To cleere his waie, whoſe lets are lawleſſe men,
And for this deede ye all ſhall be renowmd,
Renowmd and chronicled in bookes of fame,
In bookes of fame and caracters of braſſe,
Of braſſe, nay beaten golde, fight then for fame,
And finde the Arabian Muly Hamet here,
Aduenturous, bold, and full of rich reward.

*Stuk.* Braue boy, how plaine this princely mind in thee
Argues the height and honor of thy birth,
And well haue I obſeru'd thy forwardnes,
Which being tendred by your maieſtie,
No doubt the quarrell opened by the mouth
Of this yong prince vnpartially to vs,
May animate and hearten all the hoaſt,

To fight against the deuill for Lord Mahamet.
*Sebast.* True Stukley, and so freshly to my minde,
Hath this yong prince redus'd his fathers wrong,
That in good time I hope this honors fire,
Kindled alreadie with regard of right,
Bursts into open flames, and cals for warres,
Warres, warres to plant the true succeeding prince.
Lord Mahamet, I take thy noble sonne
A pledge of honor, and shal vse him so.
Lord Lodowicke, and my good Lord of Auero
See this yong prince conuaide safe to Messegon,
And there accompanide as him fitteth best,
And to this warre prepare ye more and lesse,
This rightfull warre, that Christians God will blesse.
*Exeunt.*

*Act IV*

## *Actus* 4.

*The presenter speaketh.*

Now hardned is this haplesse heathen prince,
And strengthned by the armes of Portugall,
This Moore, this murtherer of his progenie.
And warre and weapons now, and bloud and death
Wait on the counsels of this cursed king:
And to a bloudie banket he inuites
The braue Sebastian and his noble peeres.

*Enter to the bloudie banket.*

In fatall houre ariu'd this peerelesse prince,
To loose his life, his life and many liues
Of lustie men, couragious Portugals,
Drawen by ambitious golden lookes,
Let fame of him no wrongfull censure sound,

Honor

Honour was obiect of his thoughtes, ambition was
his ground. *Exit.*

*Enter Abdilmelec and his traine.* *Act IV sc. i*

*Abdilm.* Now tell mee Celybin, what doeth the e-
nemie?
*Celybin.* The enemie dread lord, hath left the towne
Of Areil, with a thouſand ſouldiers armde,
To gard his fleet of thirteene hundred ſaile,
And muſtering of his men before the wals,
He found he had two thouſand armed horſe,
And foureteene thouſand men that ſerue on foot,
Three thouſand pioners, and a thouſand cochmen,
Beſides a number almoſt numberleſſe
Of drudges, Negroes, ſlaues and Muliters,
Horſe-boies, landreſſes and curtizans,
And fifteene hundred waggons full of ſtuffe
For noble men, brought vp in delicate.
*Abdil.* Alas good king, thy fore-ſight hath bin ſmall
To come with women into Barbarie,
With landreſſe, with baggage, and with traſh,
Numbers vnfit to multiplie thy hoaſt.
*Cely.* Their paiment in the campe is paſsing ſlow,
And victuals ſcarce, that many faint and die.
*Abdilm.* But whether marcheth he in all this haſt?
*Cely.* Some thinkes he marcheth hetherward,
And meanes to take this citie of Alcazar.
*Abdil.* Vnto Alcazar, O vnconſtant chance!
*Cely.* The braue and valiant king of Portugall
Quarters his power in foure batalians,
Afront the which, to welcome vs withall,
Are ſixe and thirtie roaring peeces plaſt,
The firſt conſiſting of light armed horſe,
And of the gariſons from Tangar brought

Is lead by Aluaro Peres de Tauero,
The left or middle battell of Italians,
And Germane horſe-men Stukley doth command,
A warlike Engliſhman ſent by the pope,
That vainly cals himſelfe Marques of Ireland.
*Alonſo Aquilaz* conducts the third,
That wing of Germaine ſouldiers moſt conſiſts.
The fourth legion is none but Portugals,
Of whom Lodeuico Cæſar hath the chiefeſt charge,
Beſides there ſtand ſixe thouſand horſe
Brauely attirde, preſt where need requires.
Thus haue I tolde your roiall maieſtie,
How he is plac'd to braue his fight.

*Abdil.* But where's our nephew Muly Mahamet?

*Cely* He marcheth in the middle, garded about
With full fiue hundred hargubuze on foote,
And twice three thouſand needleſſe armed pikes.

*Zareo.* Great ſoueraigne, vouchſafe to heare me ſpeak,
And let Zareos counſell now preuaile,
Whilſt time doth ſerue, and that theſe Chriſtians dare
Approch the field with warlike Enſignes ſpread,
Let vs in haſt with all our forces meete,
And hemme them in, that not a man eſcape,
So will they be aduiſde another time,
How they doo touch the ſhore of Barbarie.

*Abdilm.* Zareo, heare our reſolution,
And thus our forces we will firſt diſpoſe,
Hamet my brother with a thouſand ſhot
On horſe-backe, and choice harguebuziers all,
Hauing ten thouſand with ſpeare and ſhield,
Shall make the right wing of the battell vp,
Zareo you ſhall haue in charge the left,
Two thouſand argolets and ten thouſand horſe,
The maine battell of harguebuze on foot,
And twentie thouſand horſe-men in their troupes,

My ſelfe inuirond with my truſtie gard
Of Ianizaries, fortunate in warre,
And toward Arzil will we take our waie,
If then our enemie will balke our force,
In Gods name let him, it will be his beſt,
But if he leuell at Alcazar wals,
Then beate him backe with bullets as thicke as haile,
And make him know and rue his ouerſight,
That raſhly ſeekes the ruine of this land.
*Exeunt.*

*Enter Sebaſtian king of Portugall, the Duke of Auero, Stukley, and others.* *Act IV sc. ii*

*Sebaſt.* Why tell me Lords, why left ye Portugall,
And croſt the ſeas with vs to Barbarie,
Was it to ſee the countrie and no more,
Or elſe to ſlay before ye were aſſaild?
I am aſhamd to thinke that ſuch as you,
Whoſe deeds haue bin renowmed heretofore,
Should ſlacke in ſuch an act of conſequence,
We come to fight, and fighting vow to die,
Or elſe to win the thing for which we came,
Becauſe *Abdilmelec* as pittying vs,
Sends meſſages to counſell quietnes,
You ſtand amaz'd and thinke it ſound aduiſe,
As if our enemie would wiſh vs anie good,
No, let him know we ſcorne his curteſie,
And will reſiſt his forces what ſo ere.
Caſt feare aſide, my ſelfe will leade the way,
And make a paſſage with my conquering ſword
Knee deepe in bloud of theſe accurſed Moores,
And they that loue my honor follow me.

Were you as reſolute as is your king,
Alcazar wals ſhould fall before your face,
And all the force of this Barbarian Lord
Should be confounded, were it ten times more.

*Auero*. So well become theſe words a kingly mouth
That are of force to make a coward fight,
But when aduice and prudent fore-ſight
Is ioynd with ſuch magnanimitie,
Troupes of victorie and kingly ſpoiles
Adorne his crowne, his kingdome, and his fame.

*Herc*. We haue deſcride vpon the mountaine tops
A hugie companie of inuading Moores,
And they my lord, as thicke as winters haile,
Will fall vpon our heads at vnawares,
Beſt then betimes t'auoide this gloomie ſtorme,
It is in vaine to ſtriue with ſuch a ſtreame.

*Enter Muly Mahamet.*

*Muly Mab*. Beholde thrice noble Lorde, vncalde I come,
To counſell where neceſsitie commands,
And honor of vndoubted victorie,
Makes me exclime vpon this daſtard flight.
Why king Sebaſtian, wilt thou now fore-ſlow,
And let ſo great a glorie ſlip thy hands?
Saie you doo march vnto Tariſſa now,
The forces of the foe are come ſo nigh,
That he will let the paſſage of the riuer,
So vnawares you will be forſt to fight.
But know O king, and you thrice valiant Lords,
Few blowes will ſerue, I aske but onely this,
That with your power you march into the field,
For now is all the armie reſolute,
To leaue the traitor helpleſſe in the fight,

And flie to me as to their rightfull prince,
Some horse-men haue alreadie lead the waie,
And vow the like for their companions,
The host is full of tumult and of feare.
Then as you come to plant me in my seate,
And to inlarge your fame in Affrica,
Now, now or neuer brauely execute
Your resolution sound and honorable,
And end this warre together with his life,
That doth vsurpe the crowne with tyrannie.
*Sebast*. Captaines, you heare the reasons of the king,
Which so effectually haue pearst wine eares,
That I am fully resolute to fight,
And who refuseth now to follow me,
Let him be euer counted cowardly.
*Auero*. Shame be his share that flies when kings do fight,
Auero laies his life before your feet.
*Stukley* For my parte Lordes, I cannot sell my bloud
Deerer than in the companie of kings.
*Exeunt.*

*Manet Muly Mahamet.*

*Muly Ma*. Now haue I set these Portugals aworke,
To hew a waie for me vnto the crowne,
Or with your weapons here to dig your graues,
You dastards of the night and Erybus,
Fiends, Fairies, hags that fight in beds of steele,
Range through this armie with your yron whips,
Driue forward to this deed this christian crew,
And let me triumph in the tragedie,
Though it be seald and honourd with my bloud,
Both of the Portugall and barbarous Moore,
Ride Nemisis, ride in thy firie cart,

And ſprinkle gore amongſt theſe men of warre,
That either partie eager of reuenge,
May honor thee with ſacrifice of death,
And hauing bath'd thy chariot wheeles in bloud,
Deſcend and take to thy tormenting hell,
The mangled bodie of that traitor king,
That ſcornes the power and force of Portugall.
Then let the earth diſcouer to his ghoſt,
Such tortures as vſurpers feele below,
Rackt let him be in proud Ixions wheele,
Pinde let him be with Tantalus endleſſe thirſt,
Praie let him be to Tiſons greedie bird,
Wearied with Siſiphus immortall toile,
And laſtly for reuenge, for deepe reuenge,
Whereof thou goddeſſe and deuiſer art,
Damnd let him be, damnd and condemnd to beare
All torments, tortures, plagues and paines of hell.

*Exit.*

*Act V* *Enter the Preſenter before the laſt dumbe ſhow, and ſpeaketh.*

Ill be to him that ſo much ill bethinkes,
And ill betide this foule ambitious Moore,
Whoſe wily traines with ſmootheſt courſe of ſpeech,
Hath tide and tangled in a dangerous warre,
The fierce and manly king of Portugall.

*Lightning and thunder.*

Nowe throwe the heauens foorth their lightning flames,
And thunder ouer Affrickes fatall fields,
Bloud will haue bloud, foul murther ſcape no ſcourge.

*Enter Fame like an Angell, and hangs the crownes vpon a tree.*

At laſt deſcendeth fame as Iris,

To finiſh fainting Didoes dying lyfe,
Fame from her ſtately bowre doth deſcend,
And on the tree as fruit new ripe to fall,
Placeth the crownes of theſe vnhappie kings,
That earſt ſhe kept in eie of all the world.

*Heere the blazing Starre.*

Now firie ſtarres and ſtreaming comets blaze,
That threat the earth and princes of the ſame.

*Fire workes.*

Fire, fire about the axiltree of heauen,
Whoorles round, and from the foot of Caſyopa
In fatall houre conſumes theſe fatall crownes,

*One fals.*

Downe fals the diademe of Portugall,

*The other fals.*

The crownes of Barbary and kingdomes fall,
Ay me, that kingdomes may not ſtable ſtand,
And now approching neere the diſmall day,
The bloudie daie wherein the battels ioyne,
Mondaie the fourth of Auguſt ſeuentie eight,
The ſunne ſhines wholy on the parched earth,
The brighteſt planet in the higheſt heauen,
The heathens eager bent againſt their foe,
Giue onſet with great ordnance to the warre.
The chriſtians with great noiſe of canon ſhot,
Send angrie onſets to the enemie.
Geue eare and heare how warre begins his ſong,
With dreadfull clamors, noiſe, and trumpets ſound.

*Exit.*

Alarums within, let the chambers be diſcharged, then enter to the battell, and the Moores flie. *Act V sc. i*

Skirmiſh ſtill, then enter Abdilmelec in his chaire, Zareo and their traine.

*Abdil.* Saie on Zareo, tell me all the newes,
Tell me what furie rangeth in our campe,

That hath inforſt our Moores to turne their backes.
Zareo ſaie, what chance did bode this ill,
What ill inforſt this daſtard cowardiſe?

*Zareo.* My Lord, ſuch chance as wilfull warre affords
Such chances and misfortunes as attend
On him, the God of battell and of armes,
My Lord, when with our ordenance fierce we ſent
Our Moores with ſmaller ſhot as thicke as haile,
Followes apace to charge the Portugall,
The valiant Duke the deuill of Auero,
The bane of Barbary, fraughted full of ire
Breakes through the rankes, and with fiue hundred horſſe
All men at armes, forward and full of might,
Aſſaults the middle wing, and puts to flight
Eight thouſand Harquebuſh that ſeru'd on foot,
And twentie thouſand Moores with ſpeare & ſheild:
And therewithall the honour of the day.

*Abdel.* Ah Abdelmelec dooſt thou liue to heare
This bitter proceſſe of this first attempt?
Labour my Lords to renue our force,
Of fainting Moores, and fight it to the laſt.
My horſſe Zareo, O the goale is loſt,
The goale is loſt, thou King of Portugall
Thrice happy chance it is for thee and thine
That heauens abates my ſtrength and calles me hence.
My ſight doth faile, my ſoule, my feeble ſoule
Shall be releaſte from priſon on this earth:
Farwell vaine world for I haue playd my parte.

He dyeth.

A long Skirmidge, and then enter his brother Muly Mahomet Seth.

*Muly.* Braue Abdelmelec, thou thriſe noble Lord,
Not ſuch a wound was giuen to Barbary,

Had

Had twenty hoaſts of men beene put to ſwoord
As death, pale death with fatall ſhaft hath giuen.
Loe dead is he, my brother and my King
Whome I might haue reuiu'd with newes I bring.

*Zareo.* His honours and his types he hath reſignde
Vnto the world, and of a manly man
Loe, in a twinckling a ſenceleſſe ſtocke we ſee.

*Muly.* You truſtie ſoldiers of this warlike King,
Be counſailde now by vs in this aduiſe,
Let not his death be bruted in the campe,
Leaſt with the ſodaine ſorrowe of the newes,
The armye wholy be diſcomfited.
My Lord Zareo thus I comforte you,
Our Moores haue brauely borne themſelues in fight
Likely to get the honour of the day
If ought may gotten be where loſſe is ſuch.
Therfore in this apparell as he dyed
My noble brother will we heere aduance
And ſet him in his chayre with cunning props,
That our Barbarians may beholde their King
And thinke he doth repoſe him in his Tent.

*Zareo.* Right pollitique and good is your aduice,
Goe then to ſee it ſpeedily performd.
Braue Lord, if Barbary recouer this,
Thy ſoule with ioy will ſit and ſee the fight.

*Exeunt.*

Alarmes. Enter to the battaile, and the chri-
ſtians flye. The Duke of A-
uero ſlaine.

*Enter Sebaſtian and Stukeley.*

*Sebaſt.* Seeſt thou not Stukley, O Stukley ſeeſt
thou not
The great diſhonour doone to Chriſtendome?

Our cheerfull onſet croſt in ſpringing hope,
The braue and mightie prince, Duke of Auero
Slaine in my fight, now ioy betide his ghoſt,
For like a lyon did he beare himſelfe.
Our battels are all now diſordered,
And by our horſes ſtrange retiring backe,
Our middle wing of foot-men ouer-rod.
Stukley, alas I ſee my ouer-ſight,
Falſe hearted Mahamet, now to my coſt,
I ſee thy trecherie, warnd to beware
A face ſo full of fraud and villanie.

Alarums within, and they runne out, and two ſet vppon Stukley, and he driueth them in.
Then enter the Moore and his boy flying.

*Moore.* Villaine, a horſe.

*Boy.* Oh my Lord, if you returne you die.

*Moore.* Villaine I ſaie, giue me a horſe to flie,
To ſwimme the riuer villaine, and to flie.

*Exit boy.*

Where ſhall I finde ſome vnfrequented place,
Some vncouth walke where I may curſe my fill,
My ſtarres, my dam, my planets and my nurſe,
The fire, the aire, the water, and the earth,
All cauſes that haue thus conſpirde in one,
To nouriſh and preſerue me to this ſhame,
Thou that wert at my birth predominate,
Thou fatall ſtarre, what planet ere thou be,
Spit out thy poiſon bad, and all the ill
That fortune, fate or heauen may bode a man.
Thou Nurſe infortunate, guiltie of all:
Thou mother of my life that broughtſt me forth,
Curſt maiſt thou be for ſuch a curſed ſonne,
Curſt be thy ſonne with euerie curſe thou haſt,
Ye Elements of whome conſiſts this clay,

This

This maſſe of fleſh, this curſed crazed corpes,
Deſtroy, diſſolue, diſturbe, and diſſipate,
What water, earth, and aire conieald.

Alarums and enter the boy.

*Boy.* Oh my Lorde, theſe rulthleſſe Moores purſue
you at the heeles,
And come amaine to put you to the ſword.
*Moore.* A horſe, a horſe, villaine a horſe,
That I may take the riuer ſtraight and flie,
*Boy.* Here is a horſe my Lord,
As ſwiftly pac'd as Pegaſus,
Mount thee thereon, and ſaue thy ſelfe by flight.
*Moore.* Mount me I will,
But may I neuer paſſe the riuer till I be
Reuengde vpon thy ſoule accurſed Abdilmelec,
If not on earth, yet when we meete in hell,
Before grim Minos, Rodamant, and Eocus,
The cumbat will I craue vpon thy ghoſt,
And drag thee thorough the lothſome pooles,
Of Lethes, Stikes, and firie Phlegiton.
*Exit.*

Alarums.
Enter Stukley with two Italians.

*Herc.* Stand traitor, ſtand ambitious Engliſh-man,
Proud Stukley ſtand, and ſtirre not ere thou die,
Thy forwardnes to follow wrongfull armes,
And leaue our famous expedition earſt,
Intended by his holynes for Ireland,
Fouly hath here betraide, and tide vs all
To ruthleſſe furie of our heathen foe,
For which as we are ſure to die,
Thou ſhalt paie ſatisfaction with thy bloud.

*Stuk.* Auant baſe villaines, twit ye me with ſhame
Or infamie of this iniurious warre?
When he that is the iudge of right and wrong
Determines battaile as him pleaſeth beſt.
But ſith my ſtarres bode me this tragicke end
That I muſt perriſh by theſe barbarous Moores,
Whoſe weapons haue made paſſage for my ſoule
That breakes from out the priſon of my breſt,
Ye proud malicious dogges of Italy
Strike on, ſtrike downe this body to the earth
Whoſe mounting minde ſtoopes to no feeble ſtroke.
Stab him.

*Ionas.* Why ſuffer we this Engliſh man to liue?
Villaine bleed on, thy blood in chanels run
And meet with thoſe whome thou to death haſt doon
*Exeunt.*

*Stuk.* Thus Stukley ſlaine with many a deadly ſtab,
Dyes in theſe deſart feilds of Affrica.
Harke freindes, and with the ſtory of my life
Let me beguile the torment of my death.
In Englands London Lordings was I borne,
On that braue Bridge, the barre that thwarts the Thames.
My golden dayes, my yonger careleſſe yeeres,
Were when I toucht the height of Fortunes wheele,
And liu'd in affluence of wealth and eaſe.
Thus in my Countrie carried long aloft,
A diſcontented humor draue me thence
To croſſe the Seas to Ireland, then to Spaine,
There had I welcome and right royall pay
Of Phillip, whome ſome call the Catholique King,
There did Tom Stukley glitter all in golde,
Mounted vpon his Iennet white as ſnowe,
Shining as Phœbus in King Phillips Court,
There like a Lord, famous Don Stukley liu'd,

For

For ſo they calde me in the Court of Spaine
Till for a blowe I gaue a Biſhops man,
A ſtrife gan riſe betweene his Lord and me,
For which, we both were baniſht by the King.
From thence, to Rome rides Stukley all a flaunt,
Receiud with royall welcomes of the Pope.
There was I grac'd by Gregorye the great,
That then created me Marquis of Ireland.
Short be my tale, becauſe my life is ſhort,
The coaſt of Italy and Rome I left.
Then was I made Leiftennant Generall
Of thoſe ſmall Forces that for Ireland went,
And with my companies embarkt at Auſtria
My Sayles I ſpred, and with theſe men of warre
In fatall houre at Liſhborne we ariu'd.
From thence to this, to this hard exigent
Was Stukley driuen to fight or els to dye,
Dar'd to the field, that neuer could endure
To heare God Mars his drum, but he muſt martch.
Ah ſweet Sebaſtian, hadſt thou beene well aduiſde
Thou mightſt haue manag'd armes ſucſeſſully.
But from our Cradles we were marked all
And deſtinate to dye in Affric heere.
Stukley, the ſtory of thy life is tolde,
Here breath thy laſt and bid thy freindes farwell.
And if thy Countries kindnes be ſo much,
Then let thy Countrie kindely ring thy knell.
Now goe, and in that bed of honour dye
Where braue Sebaſtians breathles Courſe doth lye.
Heere endeth Fortune, rule, and bitter rage:
Heere ends Tom Stukleys pilgrimage. He dyeth

Enter Muly Mahomet Seth and his traine,
with Drums and Trumpets.

*Muly*. Retreat is ſounded through our Camp, & now
From

From battells furie ceaſe our conquering Moores,
Paie thankes to heauen with ſacrificing fire,
Alcazar and ye townes of Barbarie.
Now haſt thou ſit as in a trance and ſeene,
To thy ſoules ioy and honor of thy houſe,
The trophes and the triumphs of thy men,
Great Abdilmelec and the God of kings,
Hath made thy warre ſuccesfull by thy right,
His friends whom death and fates hath tane from thee,
Lo this was he that was the peoples pride,
And cheerfull Sun-ſhine to his ſubiects all,
Now haue him hence, that roially he may
Be buried and imbalmd, as is meete.
Zareo, haue you thorough the campe proclaimd
As earſt we gaue in charge?
*Zareo.* We haue my Lorde, and rich rewardes pro-
poſde
For them that finde the bodie of the king,
For by thoſe gard that had him in their charge,
We vnderſtand that he was done to death,
And for his ſearch two priſoners Portugals
Are ſet at large to finde their roiall king.
*Muly Mah.* But of the traitrous Moore you heare
no newes.
That fled the field and ſought to ſwim the foord?
*Zareo.* Not yet my Lord, but doubtleſſe God wil tell
And with his finger point out where he hants.
*Muly Mah.* So let it reſt, and on this earth beſtow
This princely coarſe, till further for his funerals
We prouide.
*Zareo.* From him to thee as true ſucceeding prince,
With all allegeance, and with honors tipes,
In name of all thy people and thy land,
We giue this kingly crowne and diademe.
*Muly.* We thanke you all, and as my lawfull right,
With

With Gods defence and yours ſhall I keepe.

*Enter two Portugals with the bodie of the king.*

*Port.* As gaue your grace in charge, right roiall prince,
The fields and ſandie plaines we haue ſuruaide,
And euen among the thickeſt of his Lords,
The noble king of Portugall we found
Wrapt in his coulours coldly on the earth,
And done to death with many a mortall wound.
*Mab.* Lo here my Lords, this is the earth and claie,
Of him that earſt was mightie king of Portugall,
There let him lie, and you for this be free,
To make returne from hence to chriſtendome.

*Enter two bringing in the Moore.*

*One.* Long liue the mightie king of Barbary.
*Mab.* Welcome my friend, what bodie haſt thou there?
*One.* The bodie of the ambitious enemie,
That ſquandred all this bloud in Affrica,
Whoſe mallice ſent ſo many ſoules to hell,
The traitor Muly Mahamet doo I bring,
And for thy ſlaue I throw him at thy feet.
*Mab.* Zareo, giue this man a rich reward,
And thanked be the God of iuſt reuenge,
That he hath giuen our foe into our hands,
Beaſtly, vnarmed, ſlauiſh, full of ſhame,
But ſaie, how came this traitor to his end?
*One,* Seeking to ſaue his life by ſhamefull flight,
He mounteth on a hot Barbarian horſe,
And ſo in purpoſe to haue paſt the ſtreame,
His headſtrong ſtead throwes him from out his ſeate,
Where diuing oft for lacke of ſkill to ſwim,

It was my chance alone to ſee him drownd,
Whom by the heeles I dragd from out the poole,
And hether haue him brought thus filde with mud.
*Mab.* A death too good for ſuch a damned wretch,
But ſith our rage and rigor of reuenge,
By violence of his end preuented is,
That all the world may learne by him to auoide,
To hall on princes to iniurious warre,
His ſkin we will be parted from his fleſh,
And being ſtifned out and ſtuft with ſtrawe,
So to deterre and feare the lookers on,
From anie ſuch foule fact or bad attempt,
Awaie with him.
And now my Lords, for this chriſtian king,
My Lord Zareo, let it be your charge,
To ſee the ſouldiers tread a ſolempne march,
Trailing their pikes and Enſignes on the ground,
So to performe the princes funeralls.

*Here endeth the tragicall battell of Alcazar.*

CPSIA information can be obtained
at www.ICGtesting.com
Printed in the USA
BVHW01s0427210118
505873BV00010B/395/P

9 780649 340507